THE LOST CAFETERIA

THE L■ST CAFETERIA

JOEL ROBERT FERGUSON

CLARISE FOSTER, EDITOR

EDITIONS

© 2020, Joel Robert Ferguson

All rights reserved. No part of this book may be reproduced, for any reason, by any means, without the permission of the publisher.

Cover design by Doowah Design.
Cover art: "Untitled"(orange, grey, white, and black cut-up composition), 2016, by Mark McKinnon.
Photo of Joel Ferguson by Z L Raymond.

This book was printed on Ancient Forest Friendly paper.
Printed and bound in Canada by Marquis Book Printing.

We acknowledge the support of The Canada Council for the Arts and the Manitoba Arts Council for our publishing program.

Library and Archives Canada Cataloguing in Publication

Title: The lost cafeteria / Joel Robert Ferguson ; Clarise Foster, editor.
Names: Ferguson, Joel Robert, 1985- author. | Foster, Clarise, 1955- editor.
Description: Poems.
Identifiers: Canadiana 20200184393 | ISBN 9781773240640 (softcover)
Classification: LCC PS8611.E739 L68 2020 | DDC C811/.6—dc23

Signature Editions
P.O. Box 206, RPO Corydon, Winnipeg, Manitoba, R3M 3S7
www.signature-editions.com

for Anne

1

THE KITCHEN DEBATES

Capacity	11
Walking Backwards	13
Twenties	15
Rucksack Elegy	16
The Kitchen Debates, Early-to-Mid 2008	17
Riding Freight	18
Shooting Guns with the Europeans	19
Bughouse	21
An Economy Like Any Other	23
A Few Train-Hoppers	25
Quickening Cities	27
A Directory of Enchanted Trash	28

2

CLOSED SPACE

Shunpiking	32
On Site Over Surface	33
After Turner's Stags	34
Boxing Day at the Fort Garry Palm Lounge	35
Ghost Hunting at the Ninette Sanitorium	36
The Folly Arch	37
Historical Drama	38
Halifax: Colonial Shards	40
Percocet on Election Night, 2016	46
Aubade of the Oprichniki	47
The Hôtel Universel	49
Apartment Hunting near the Jolicoeur Metro	50
Maud Lewis Houses	51
Night Roads, Long Exposure	53
Closed Space, 1988	54
Distance, Love, Sum	55
Common Coin	56
Paris Syndrome in New York	59

3

THE LOST CAFETERIA

Whitehorse, Yukon Territory, New Year's Morning	62
On-the-Job Braining	64
Nightsoil	65
Downtown After Dessert	66
Spring Without End	67
Cool Universe	68
The Lonely Numerous	69
Tower Block Cleaner	70
Creatures of the Field	72
Moon Poem for Coleridge	73
Something Yet Deserves to Live	74
Rush Our Bus	75

4

SWEETER THRU DIFFICULTIES

Ora et Labora	78
The Berlin Wall, Again and Again	79
His Whitetails at the Northern Shore	80
A Catalogue Mandolin	82
Bed Leaves Red Fall	84
The News	85
The Eschatongues	86
Bona Fide Masters	88
Head in the Clouds	89
Patch Work	90
The White Horse	92
Continental	94

Notes	96
Acknowledgements	97

1

THE KITCHEN DEBATES

Capacity

A friend of a friend from out west
comes calling to the verdant college town
where I live like a bandit king, where I drink
wine made from dumpstered apricots by a stone bridge
over the Speed River (or was it the Eramosa?)
I read Max Stirner, pack on
ill-gotten weight eating stolen wheels of brie.
I've forged a new aristocratic, deadbeat identity
while the Southern Ontario summer sprawls
leans into farmland, stretches its arms and yawns.
I have sticky fingers. I smell of rot.
I believe I am happy. I'm probably not.

I never meet him. He leaves
his backpack on my porch, heads downtown
decides to swim the Eramosa
or perhaps the Speed. He's young and able
and a chance current buries him
like a blade deep in the river.

I walk the gravel paths of the Eramosa
and Speed that night— calling out
a name I have no face for,
the ritual to conjure life.

What rise instead are Latin names
for rare diseases that singled out classmates
in the first-world backwater of my childhood.
I return to the small-town, non-denominational
services for the silent girl from math class
loved fiercely by a few close friends,
for the high school principal's outgoing son,
his football teammates in the front pews.

I resurrect the yearly contractions
of extended families, elderly neighbours
who fell into black-hole retirement homes. A friend
lost her father in preschool: assuring everyone
how little she thought of him
set the rhythm for her nervous tics. The sick
and old became less themselves
in well-mapped increments. Surviving
was within their capacity, until it wasn't.

All of this followed naturally, in stages
with grief counsellors and pamphlets at every milestone—
reading from their scripts made sense of life.
The spell breaks with morning. He is found
downstream a span, tangled in the town's
flotsam. I see the gurney
they carry him away on, the black sheet
that covers him. What remains, awaits—
his army-green rucksack on the stoop
with its boundary-stone weight.

Walking Backwards

after Joe Brainard

I remember heading downtown on the eighteen
                how at Selkirk and Main
my phone shuffled onto some old song
and the early morning light suddenly dazzled me.

I remember business-sponsored street art
covering up off-sales and pawnshops
like broken-down salarymen
forced to wear party hats.

I remember photocopies of train schedules
Canadian Pacific crew-change locations
vague directions on getting there from the highway.

I remember you and me breaking
into a falling-down cottage by the lake
but can't say which of us fell asleep first.

I remember taking a Sharpie
to draw a big rococo-looking gateway
around the window overlooking the tracks
(a gesture to endings and false starts, I think).

I remember you and me standing sheepish
by the train when the engine workers saw
us trying to find rideable cars,
that train heading north without us.

I remember the butterflies
waiting for that next one
and having to piss every five minutes (nerves).

I remember hitchhiking to Sudbury alone.

I remember old Spanish Loyalists
speaking at anarchist bookfairs.

I remember my first hit of acid
and writing gibberish about Heidegger.

I remember taking toboggans
to Ford Needham Memorial Park with friends
whose contact info is now long lost.

I remember photos from after garage shows—
twenty sweaty teenagers, punks and goths
giving their small-town best with impeccable hair.

I remember "Might as well go for a soda,
nobody hurts, nobody cries" (Kim Mitchell)
and how being straight-edge made one feel above it all.

I remember mosh pits, elbows,
noses, jets of red, red blood
at the Legion, teenhood's
broken-nosed jubilance.

I remember that Victoria Park closes at ten
to fill with creeping small-town cops
trying to nab pot-head kids and dudes cruising.

Mostly though I remember overnight trains
in my bedroom window as a kid—
sleeping travellers heading elsewhere
in a golden flash of light.

Twenties

Uprooting for a crush was simple at nineteen:
the sharehouse fridge still full of vegetable salvage,
my last twenty got me off the island.

Cresting on uppers, the long-haul driver
outside Rivière-du-Loup grew suspicious,
called me a narc when I copped to being
a Nova Scotian who'd never been to Cape Breton.
Too many short rides later, Yves the travelling jeweller
dropped me off in a warehouse district and the rain,
a two-hour walk to my new home.

Of the crush's roommates, one plotted a move to Germany
where gay wrestling leagues sprang up like fistfuls of flowers.
The other was a law student and activist, remaking the world
as a federation of communes from behind his germaphobe's mask
in the age of Swine Flu, in the afterglow of SARS.
Third night there, she let me in on her love
for him (the masked man, not the wrestler)
while we filled army-surplus rucksacks with dumpstered beets.

Their bedrooms flanked mine,
and the Saint John River had no dishes for me
to wash (no work, no deliverance).
I waited a week in the nest I'd made
out of blankets and sci-fi paperbacks,
rolling dimes in sunspots on matted hardwood floors.

I didn't want to die so much,
just silently joked about which room
leaving my body in would make the biggest splash—
but the highway was just a two-hour walk away
and besides, it was my birthday.

Beginnings were still as easy at twenty,
chopping wood, clearing deadfall
for friendly strangers one province east of it all
for two days and five twenty-dollar bills.

Rucksack Elegy

Most things are left out and what isn't
takes on its proper dimensions.

Essentials and irreplaceables only:
wool socks, trail mix, letters (love

or otherwise) formed into a cube
by gravity and canvas and fastened

to the torso. A seat while waiting, pillow
in highway-side underbrush come dark,

ready for most anything. Sturdy too,
when tossed from a freight train

slowly pulling into a railyard,
its fall gauging speed and safety

for its owner who waits to follow.
Laid over in unknown cities,

it stretches sufficiency just that
little bit further for the lived road

movie, the pastoral painting,
a clumsy joke finding its moment.

The Kitchen Debates, Early-to-Mid 2008

Other people's suburban kitchens existed for us
to put anything which our paws could muster
up our noses, for forgetting
a thieved Ted Hughes omnibus in (forever),
to walk from talking to rustle up booze
and to never come back to.

Talked walking down the tracks in Southern Ontario
ganging-way to let late GO Transit trains go,
their double-decker windows
fishbowls in the snow.
Debate frothing about the Chiapas,
Italian Autonomists, Alfredo Bonanno.
Conclusion: *of course* the state must go.

A giddy, addled gestalt kicking down
the back door of another half-finished trackside
bungalow abandoned mid-sentence, like it was owed
to encroaching war, the first
of many more in the crashing months to follow.

In this pad's other rooms, comrades, sex for them.
as for me, Pasternak and Dexedrine,
a kitchen sink to piss in and a carpeted basement
for sleep. Who would need more?

What times to live thru! Pockets and backpack
compartments filled at the supermarket
before the housing bust, then go-go-go!
Seven white smiles, then mine, piling
into someone's mum's minivan
with Subcommandante Marcos,
the Years of Lead,
Alfredo Bonanno.

No volta here, no tears
for a lost generation, just petty crime brazening.

Riding Freight

adrift on a line   revering machine precision   bearing our lives slowly

thru interchanges   around blind corners
causeways across muskeg   mile markers
where mottled bits of dross float
            plastic bags in dead trees   the only sign of civilization
                    unseen   lulled on by the rhythm of this stillness

open-air metal coffins   the porches of grain cars
grime and soot   the smell of grease following us thru city
                                                upon city, rail yards
hushed by the bull's flashlight
the yard worker's high beams

in the name of this world's sovereign   (Capital)

a night of wilderness remains
blank to us above   the plains oh lord
at rest   at a siding   lightning (purple and gold) on all horizons

to emerge hundreds of miles later   the trick pulled off   unscathed

                                        grounded

Shooting Guns with the Europeans

There's a cock-up with the packing house machinery
        so a rare day off bisects the cherry harvest.

    Why don't we go shoot some guns?

      The Europeans follow Country Boy's pickup
in a rattling, rusted-out Astrovan, its body a patchwork
      of spray can dregs. Here they come—
      Florence, Greenwich, Heidelberg, Prague.
      They keep pace with the truck, careening
thru every blind turn and switchback on our ascent
to the shooting-copse, while the mountains of the Okanagan
      hold their breath and turn a deeper blue.

The Europeans park and scatter, dreadlocked,
jocular and slap-happy, boxing with their shadows. Country Boy's
the youngest here by a span, a local among come-from-aways,
generous with his licence and guns, the small trap
      and box of clay pigeons last heard skittering
      around the flatbed like an ad hoc bonspiel.
Taking a knee to set up the launcher, he rises
         an adult, extolling gun safety basics
         as the Europeans sip cider on the tailgate
         and paw the dirt, eager for gunplay.

We try blasting the pigeons down, taking five shots each.
The best first-timer among us is the only woman.
      She brings each bird to ground
with fitting neophyte gravitas, but European smirks fly
like oratory on the last pull that wonkily veers hard left,
her barrel tracking it in a sweeping arc but missing.

No one is shocked when they change into wolves. One moment
the Europeans play at war, firing wildly at stumps and road signs,
         taking videos of each other, little kids
         pushing every button on the elevator to feel
the power of their clumsy fingers over the wide world, then—
         tails and snouts, crazed yellow eyes
they bolt thru the underbrush and up along the ridge.

We never find them, just traces— retirees' lapdogs
that disappear from fenced-in yards to turn up on trails,
throats ripped out, and the yammer-yowled threats bouncing down
from the hills before dawn to mark their presence,
        walking parallel to us
        towards a future made for carnivores.

Bughouse

...the blizzard the bedbugs the bastard landlord
is too cheap to spray for all deserve each other
and we haven't hit december yet... we are weary
from the outset doorways become jammed
with ice the one window that gets some sunlight
shattered by the settling of the house garbage
bags taped to window frame rippling in the arctic
breeze... the social sphere shrinks and the walls amplify
every sound too many friends paying too much
rent for too few rooms the whole rotting place
becomes one high-register piano key they take turns jabbing
harder and harder... it's the least-bad option

it isn't even the goddamn new year yet... another winter
spent stacking empties bingeing
on television and self-reproach spent scratching
bug bites and waiting for the world
or the weather to pull a u-turn escalating
screaming fits scandal over small things
speculation around who is going to fuck over who
on the lease come spring... frequent trips
down icy streets to the psych ward a ten-ring circus
juggling prescriptions and crises...
resilience is now a weasel-word
that everyone's grown tired of just makes them think
of bedbugs those bloodsuckers will persist
beyond the heat-death of the universe... and yet

the latest traveller from bughouse to bughouse
sneaks her visitor a baked potato
from her tray he eats it slowly and draws a promise
from her that she'll bring him some of those ill-fitting
blue denim shirts the attendants make her wear
a genuflection to all her tomorrows a sound request
because all his clothes have been sprayed with raid
and he can't take them out of the garbage bag
for another two weeks... everyone would prefer
winter to be over the words *kindness*
decency respite we would prefer
to thrive... so we cling
to the moments when we can still cope
with each other...

An Economy Like Any Other

Traded *Les Fleurs du Mal* for *Nine Stories*
to S on ferry from Caribou to Prince Edward Island
as dolphins paced us and crossed the tack.
A real bad trade. He turned up
a couple weeks later at my house, dropped acid
made a pass at a roommate—
shot down, he ran off naked into the night.

Traded *Discipline & Punish*
for *Gramsci is Dead* to E
at some collective in downtown Kingston.
Confused, I thought I was getting
Let's Spit on Hegel. What else to say?

Traded *No Great Mischief*
for some essays by Mary Baker Eddy
(why do I do this to myself?)
to a sweet old Christian Scientist
on the train to Montreal.
She left before the blizzard that brought
and prolonged the night.

Traded *A Place in the Country*
(Essays on German Romanticism)
for Zamyatin's *We* to M
in London (England not Ontario!)
We also traded postcards and photographic evidence
of all things pedestrian from Tbilisi to Tofino.

Received C's copy of *Paterson*
with scorch marks
from a dropped match
imprinted on the cover
just like a muskellunge
trying to leap
the image of the falls
and continue
up the Passaic.

Abandoned Hemingway, Gogol, Red Emma,
to the driveway of a burnt home
while hitchhiking, outside Saint-Nicolas, Quebec.
Forgive me this offering, I was
dehydrated and not thinking clearly.

A Few Train-Hoppers

A ragged, xeroxed zine
spews its pages
from the gondola into
the woods five minutes
past Rivière-du-Loup,
its directions, symbols
and schedules. So expires
the hidden story's
statute of limitations.
        […]
(another junker
fresh air, kinda)
        […]
("no, my dog loves it,
this life on the rails")
        […]
(Dodging the Charny bull,
his mirror on a stick,
living to tell the tale
to those who'd lived it
already. Or not–)
        […]
(secondhand story–
flail-handy, sloppy
drunk, vaporized, pissed,
eviscerated, riding suicide,
blowing up the squat)
        […]
(A last-summer type of friend
in the word-of-mouth streets.
Faint-faced, distant-eyed,
hard lines glazed on whatever,
cute liddle cupcake
last year. Nod of recognition
then gone forever.)
        […]

(Tamped weeds, snipped
fence, waiting with bag wine
under some now-bulldozed
Vendome overpass. The horizon's
endless, especially
where it isn't.)
        [...]
That's what it's like,
that thing about secrets
passed on mouth to ear,
the feeling that keeps getting
traipsed 'round: nostalgia
without regression (almost).

Quickening Cities

While buried in Turgenev on an overground train
there are the glass towers of course, but also
the Anglosphere shade of Roque Dalton
lingering in a third-storey bookstore or the Sun
Yat-Sen memorial garden most afternoons. Each lost face
waits on Commercial Drive with its dog, ready
with a mickey of whiskey to freshen my Slurpee.
Whichever continental philosopher hated the city's countless
locked doors has been reincarnated as a janitor
with the master keys. The singing cowboy of yesteryear
still fills my mug with joe in the Bon's on Broadway
of memory. The deluge lifts
off from the flooding and moves
northwards. Drunk-punks like cherubim hold up
a SpongeBob beach towel for a girl who changes
to a girl-plus-one in Grandview Park. Keeping cold,
the mountains trade in baldnesses. What is it about
last year's snow, Franky-boy? I watch
an East Berliner face his acrophobia
among a score of newborns on the Grouse Mountain
      cable car—   this other city
coming thru with the dawn sun's
slow moments commuting towards Autumn,
Portage and Main.

A Directory of Enchanted Trash

for Riley & Janis

So long safe haven, first home
found in young adulthood's approximation
punk-house we all outgrew at last coming to rest.

Thirteen years of handing off the lease
from friend to friend of friend and so on
comes down to this—
                                frantically gutting
the house in the final hours before the first of the month
sweating with the signatory in the damn Manitoban heat
for a sniff at the damage deposit
long after the last subletter skimped on cleaning,
split with hamster cage in hand
before the absentee landlord at last makes his appearance.

Someone always will, for someone must:
slap-patch wall-holes, re-set the doors
find a buyer to pick up both fridges for cheap
clean the wall of mirrors and the Doric column
put in by the old pianist who lived here previous.

Empty the shelves and cupboards,
drag submerged relics from the black mould basement,
form a directory of our enchanted trash
in piles on the front lawn.
Lay out the mementos of kids running away
from evangelizing families, dead towns and instrumental reason:
photos with face tattoos, highways or riding freight,
posters for punk bands forgotten by the clouds and streams,
thank-you-for-your-hospitality letters
with reciprocal invites to look them up
on the coast next fall (a decade ago).

Break up the piano that came with
the place with a hatchetful of chutzpah,
just eviscerate the beast—
slow motion blade-falls golden
in the extended play of back lane prairie sunset.
Load the soundboard into a van
borrowed from a friend's mum
and head towards the city dump, that magic mountain
where sloughed-off worlds form middens.
To the curb with the rest:
we lived with it all for as long as we could stand it.

2

CLOSED SPACE

Shunpiking

Hottest day of August. I'm on the apartment's roof
thinking about what I've been reading
—Egon Schiele   Spanish Flu
last days of the Hapsburgs
1918   the end of the war
culture   high and low
                    "last words"—

but mostly just watching the traffic pass
below, thinking about how little I want
to walk back to the laundromat, when
a jeep guns and swerves thru a red
at the corner of Windsor and North.

Cursing from shotgun, a muscle-man half stands
in his seat to make a throwing gesture and, yes,
something glints an arc thru humid air
from his hand to an unseen resting place.

They roar off down the road, only
to return moments later in the oncoming lane
mounting the curb. Excitable tank-topped boys
hop out, scour thru the grass
outside the leftie magazine office next door.

It's so hot that everything's melting,
leaving gaps where I catch glimpses
of Vienna thru the sweat
palaces that look like ornate cakes

while below they look, dig, look,
and the one who tossed away
his wedding band cries
into his phone, asking for her forgiveness.

On Site Over Surface

the red-flecked barn
the baseball arcs up
and down the roof
back to glove or to ground
       at last crests over shingles to come
down behind the neighbour's fence

elsewhere out of mind
       patchy lumps of green grass
hide the dent a septic tank inhabited
       and the burial grounds surrounding

no amphora's handle here
thru the soil's roils
       troubled stones
       coins and bones

and thru numbered days
of sash window squares
next to 1890's buggy calendar
       faded patches of george v
       still affixed *in situ*
look out at wreckage wrought
by the ball among the
                raspberries.

After Turner's Stags

I see a clutch of red and fallow, all
enclosed off-canvas. Day chases night
with a can of black and tan,
while jumbo jets float
in the pink of a bad year, caught
in marmalade above Gatwick.

Sweltering Brits! Long grass spills
down the slope. Robust regard
for parks but sold out of cornettos.
Again and again explained a drive to flee
for Kent, Galloway, Somerset, the din somewhere
waves crash into stone lions' cliff-carved maws.

Polyphemus is in the next chamber, his father stirring.
The rubber map of an old port's streets I leave
as giants grind down to enjoy feeling
a city squish beneath heel. Fairy-rings
are sprouting around Saint Paul's.
Underwater tunnels are the last damp place, cool,
the Thames' old bricks quivering green jelly.

The point of dogs to Turner's at-bay stags.
The roars are hollowed,
weather no polite conversation
when an age of aftermath arrives. Two centuries on,
Greenwich, I didn't mean it. Straw hats,
subscription lawn chairs should take note.

Boxing Day at the Fort Garry Palm Lounge

Well, the ghosts are locked in their hotel rooms,
          or hotel room closets, and the botanical gardens
                    have been knocked down, their centennial ficuses
          and turtles are gone. The palms left to us as a city
are those patterned into the carpet of the Palm Lounge:
          the rest is ice chunks and hypothermia.

                    Worst snowfall since '87, I keep hearing.
Hours spent wrangling a snowblower thru downtown drifts
          until I can track slush across the fine lobby floor,
                              regress into whatever pricey cocktail
          I remember Don Draper ordering. The interior
is all gilt imperial, the brass-buttoned
waiter in his Kim Jong-Un coat chatty.
          He has a strong union, his name is Dave
there are sealed-off tunnels below the hotel, a settler cave-town,
                    he's making time-and-a-half bank this Boxing Day.

          The pianist's off to Chicago to see family.
          Billy Joel will have to wait 'til the new year.
Scarce-to-gone, too, are the Easterners, Yanks,
German tourists roaming about for a peek
          at the necessarily-lost world of vaulted ceilings. The locals
would come to play tourist among them while they (the tourists)
waited for their westbound train to let them back on,
continue on Cornelius Van Horne's Edwardian El Dramino
at the lounges of Chateau Lake Louise or The Empress.

                    Light fails fast here now
                    and a thigh-high slog home
                    in bitter cold is the evening's chaser.

Ghost Hunting at the Ninette Sanitorium

Down the stairs
from wreckage to ruin
I feel the absence
of a presence at my elbow.

Something's about to begin.
Goosebumps. Electric.
Breath held. Any moment now.

Twenty bucks a gander:
the brown grass outlines outbuildings' foundations,
a fear of TB lingers in negative.
No footsteps to ruffle the asbestos
dust in the main ward's attic
locked thirty years until this morning
the caretaker says. It's her birthday
and the spirits are whiffs of vodka:
we ought to have brought masks.

A search for meaning in malfunctioning light
switches, creaky floors, resonance, miasmic
dis-ease. *Does a life have to end for a ghost to begin?*

We recover them later, back in the city—
photographed, smiling in sepia
lined up in their beds
along the balcony and behind them all
a white coat and glinting spectacles.
Aunts, grandparents, progenitors who passed
thru the San
hang around
families' forks and branches
smile and pace in the background
haunt the tall grass
stick to the burrs that stuck to us.

The Folly Arch

I   step aside   gangway
out of London   South Western Rail
boot sale   regalia
fallen from the lorry   laid
in a polyglot field   mugs
to commemorate royal marriages
          now long-dissolved
past pubs   thru two villages
the ring road asleep   the islands
small when all's added up
               stone steps
old growth shade   footpaths
around great craters
dug up   no doubt by
German bombs   out
into June heat   the farmers' wilting
fields   hedgerows   a riding
lesson   and into vision

          the arch from Thomas More's time

fenced off for farthings
          that childhood scuttlebutt
placed under bricks   five centuries'
waifish deconstruction
          the foundations of
a house beneath feet   above
winds in Gobions Wood
               still the green-sea
the utopia left over
from some dead lord's
garden   come clearance
enclosure   some googled stone
bridge wrapped in bluebells
under repair   cannot find it
cannot approach   trust that it's there
in the glow of what years remain to us

Historical Drama

Water laps.
Boat creaks.
Footsteps rustle thru leaves.
Horn bellows.
Rhythmic drumming.

the mercy of the old stories
recognizing their conclusions
as present consequences

Festive chatter and laughter.
Cutlery clatters.
Doors burst open.
Flames whoosh.
Ominous howling.
Footsteps scuff.
Log clunks.
Flames roar.
Startled gasps.
Relieved sigh.

warm screens   familiar folk
the bog-standard glow of childhood
dance of cathode shadows   den of memory
before the responsibility to know begins

Birds chirp.
Laboured whispers.
Wheezing.
Men chatter and laugh.
Drunken sighs.
Horse whinnies nearby.
Rain patters.
Kissing, sighing with pleasure.
Harness jingles, goats bleat.
Wagon rattles as it trundles away.
Wailing. Gut-wrenching sobs.

go back to whatever beginning
I was small   the world was small with me
after nature   before culpability
no log cabin in a dark wood to revisit
a golden age   an infantile disorder

Loud thunderclap.
Heartbeat pulses loudly.
Men scream in agony.
Fighting grunts.
Warrior yells.
Weapons clank.
Gurgling grunt.
Hard blow.

today's nightmare made fodder
tomorrow's period pieces
boltholes for Pangloss   carnage naturalized
made bearable   inevitable   a good

Grunts of effort.
Flames crackle and roar.
Ragged breathing.
Blood splatters.

Halifax: Colonial Shards

after "Viking Dublin: Trial Pieces" by Seamus Heaney

I

Perhaps these are the bones
of those stolen, enslaved, or protestants
called foreign, mercenaries from Westphalia;
anyhow, an open pit

was dug, a vessel now
beneath the church's abutments.
Like a shaggy-dog story
spilling the bounds

of its purview,
like a child's game,
old-fashioned, pick-up sticks,
the city forgets itself,

flying from the hands
that first raised it,
shackles daisy-chained,
ragged sets of lungs.

II

These are expected shards,
the buried stories
returning to haunt:
kidnappings, bounties,

plague ships explicated
by tangled roots
of stone and bone,
which in the breach

retrace their anabasis
so that each brainpan
is a wide-bellied ship
crowning out of Halifax harbour,

past expedience and assault,
remembering the path
from Demina, Dahomey,
Hesse, Hamburg, Cologne.

III

Like wet gunpowder
spilled across abandoned
acreage allotments,
the boneyard in bloom

just beyond the palisade,
that charged limit
bloody and final as when
Cornwallis first said *scalps*.

And so now we hear
from students on the dig,
the codex of femurs,
the twice-buried men:

and from these test fragments
inscribed by Great Empires,
a pilgrim ship the hydra's tooth
today springs from.

IV

Here this imitation falters,
didactic, unravelling
into the semaphore of concern,
the common coin of white guilt

at a remove from the material.
I write "I am Bartolomé de las Casas,"
turn moralist, truism-mouther,
one of the good ones

making the demanded judgments
of the dead and of history.
Pinioned by a greed
to be beyond reproach,

pious and useless,
rolling around on this
and that burial mound
like a mutt in the sun.

V

I get on with it,
shut-in student
trying to reach terms with
the ancestors who lived on:

broad-gaited, notch-hilted
killers, rangers
and *Landsknechte*, ten-guinea men,
agents of pain and terror,

who gained notoriety or respect
working to carve title and deed
in the growing neighbourhoods,
who time transmuted into the names

of streets, schools, statues.
Old names that cling to the now,
that dig down deep into my bones
like a thoughtless pride.

VI

"And here you will see
where three hundred bodies
were stacked head to heel,
forgotten for two centuries

under the Little Deutsch Church,
until renovations in the lead-up
to Helmut Kohl's G7 visit."
Would the tour guides who patrol

pecuniary neighbourhoods say this
if a key market wasn't kept moving
by the engine of storytelling,
tales quaint and easy to grasp?

The words slip around
submerged crafts, dig up
fragments of ignorance (my own)
from within the stratified earth.

Percocet on Election Night, 2016

Sent home with kidney stones and a script for pills,
the pain is replaced with the sense that I'm one
of William Blake's paintings, little boy lost
done, gone, bedbound
as the whirlwind comes unwound.

I eat painkillers in reams,
prognosticate lies,
hopeful about the shard pressing hard upstream.
By the john I watch myself sick.
I fire codeine in a golden stream.

Sisyphus is now carefree from his burden,
drifting thru the patriot colours
and analyses of the live-streamed verdict.

In the dream I'm breaking
all of Blake's plates. My body is
both banks of the river,
a Quisling on the make.

The world is my pillow. Like a haze
I rise out the window, then on
and on. I'm a scroll unfurled in the sky
over Spain. I glide above Guernica.
What's below is ablaze
but I'm at rest, well past dawn on day zero
well beyond healthy or ill.
At the bereft heart of heart's deficit
Percocet won't wake me
to anything harsh just yet.

Aubade of the Oprichniki

███████ nurses a grudge— Someone has cut him
off on the road. Someone has sure done ████ wrong. ████ doesn't
like the look of Someone's face. ████ is drawn to Someone
and hates Someone for it. ████ knows
Someone has stabbed The People in the back.

Come, oh come, day when The Word is given,

speak, speak, speak the sentence!

A fear of shrinking and blowing away
consumes ██████ .
██ is tired of the bills and purposeless drudge.
████ thrills to think of kicking Someone down the street.
██ hates distant relations and burns for familial killings.
The Eye craves, Eye wants the viscera of abject reality.

The World has broken, The World will be fixed; the past's purity is a truncheon.
The Voice speaks the words that ██████ knows and that Someone dreads.

Tell, tell, tell and keep on telling.

The Law is given, The Word is taken, yes,

speak, speak, speak the sentence!

Eye has an escape from the quotidian
a purity of purpose from naming
Someone The Enemy. ████ takes
up a mask of red, ████ a mask of white.
They come snickering to Someone's dwelling
and drag Someone from bed. Yes,

**to Someone's house came dreaded guests,
axes danced upon their head!**

███ ██ ███ & ████

take a cue from ████ 's laughter
in the night. ████ holds the rope that drags Someone
by the neck and thru the mud. ████
merrily throws a child-sized Someone from the upstairs window.

The gates split down the middle, down the middle!
Golden goblets are passed from hand to hand!

The play of work is finished,
The Eye takes it in and enjoys it all: the degradation
of Someone destroyed, the smell of burning crossbeams
the royal blue of the coming of dawn
the killers' laughter as they sing their morning song.

The Hôtel Universel

A ziggurat of all that's best for only the best, the guests
are dry and well-fed. The wedding on the mezzanine level

is one to remember for all in attendance, but the halls above
are cold and silent. After the front desk formalities, no one's asked

for their papers, and the beds are so large that nobody touches
if they don't want to. The pizzeria the concierge suggests

gets so many orders wrong, sends every room extra anchovies
that perfume the halls with the sea and death, but a woman's kind voice

will dispatch apologies and free pizzas with an accent
that can't quite be placed. At the Hôtel Universel

no one feels transient, and not in an unsettling way either—
it's just that none of the pens bearing the hotel's logo have ink

so one's thoughts keep escaping out into the drizzly night.
The wi-fi is patchy too, but you can still stream

Frozen or *The Shining*, if you don't mind the pauses to buffer
that extend and silence the closeup of Danny's silent scream.

Apartment Hunting near the Jolicoeur Metro

The break you catch at last is not yours. It's the rentier's,
it is psychotic. Since the photos were taken for Kijiji,
the white walls have been lovingly swabbed black and red
and a pentagram's been carved into the coffee table.

He rambles about the book he's writing on Satan,
the Kingdoms of Hell, the Transmigration of Souls;
names an ever-rising price, but lets slip hidden fees.

Continuing the tour, he presents the kitchen,
appliances pawned. The backyard is overgrown.
The zeitgeist has been captured in the plastic bureau
housing the rats he bred to keep his pet snake fed.
He says there's only two rats left. The snake is dead.

You say you'll contact him, soon, and hurry back
to the Metro. The day's housing crisis aside,
doubling what's broken does not make it whole.

Maud Lewis Houses

House #1

You see the replica first—
a wee, shed-sized thing,
white with green and red
trim. The summer morning's
       light and the dew
       on the grass in your approach
       make you feel young as when
       the world was new. But in your eagerness
you have arrived early and cannot enter
this copy of her life. The tourist centre in Digby
is open, so you buy a mug
with a winter scene printed on it. Belled oxen
       pull their sledges thru a world
       without shadows within the wrapping paper.

        House #2

    In your rented red convertible, you drive
    twenty minutes down the Evangeline Trail
    to see the memorial. Another scale replica
    of Maud Lewis's house stands uncomfortably close
    to the highway, in the glade where the genuine article
    once stood. This copy is made from unpainted steel,
    its ashy surfaces lifeless and cold, reminding you
    of the skyscrapers in the big city you left behind.
    No, you don't like it, this tiny metal box shorn
    of every ingenuous element. You leave quickly,
    not waiting for years of salt-water vapours
    to rust this monument back into innocence.

Third & Final House

Her original resides inside the Art Gallery of Nova Scotia now—
the provincial government purchased it after she died
and moved it here in the eighties. Hurry thru the other
exhibits to arrive at her true home, your excitement growing. Here it is,
nestled in the corner of a gaping room, a handful of quilt
still hot from the dryer, clutched loosely in a treasure-laden hand.
The door is open for you. Pass inside. You half-expect—
what? Her to be alive within, at work, small as the last
of a nesting-doll sequence? Or perhaps to find her body
laid out for a viewing, miraculously preserved, an influx
of peasants steadily coming to do homage, touching her
crooked hands, praying to be cured? But no, there is only you,
stooped low by her ceiling, the only beating heart within your chest.
The colours she laid on every surface of this humblest home run riot.
Blooms shoot across the walls, the table, the cast-iron stove,
the rustic crockery the gallery nailed to the countertop.
Wonder that any life exists outside her home at all, so total,
vital, all-devouring the paints at play within this house.

You are returned from your reverie by the television
that's been mounted on the back wall. A documentary loops,
the black-white-grey of the screen so out of place here.
Until recently, she sold hand-painted Christmas cards
to local sophisticates for five dollars apiece, the narrator explains
as she paints a harbour scene.
                                        Leave her creation now,
having seen that which you've come to see, and glow
with a satisfaction that will remain with you
after the return to your home in the world.

Night Roads, Long Exposure

for Maeve

Pull back the camera, the tripod,
the body from the freight train's path.

Foothills winter in condensation
rising from trickling rocks. A general   *the folly cut*
store in the woods, the husk of a world
today's ventures won't fill. Churches,   *o lord, antecedent*
farmhouses conceded atop hills are painted
time and again to adorn retirement homes.
Here a residential school left ablaze,   *shubenacadie*
a village named for old barns abandoned
when redcoats came, somehow standing   *same*
decades before joining the common litany.

Here are cabins left behind, photo albums intact,   *kemptown*
an airstrip's guardian the lonely chain slack   *debert*
across broken concrete, an old highway's moon-channels—
and over rime-crusted roads, you
with camera, plastic bags in shoes, the night being yours,   *still*
frame forms to endure the negatives.

Closed Space, 1988

An early dream or memory—
the end of the sci-fi horror show,
on the big tv-as-furniture *Zenith*,
past bedtime at a relative's house.
An old man, wild white hair
inventor and/or victim
is tricked into his glass coffin
by a rogue computer, or jealous brother.
A needle (poison? embalming fluid?) jabs him.
The actor emotes pain and howling-terror.
I watch as open palms strike the lid.
The glass box starts rolling on its own
(the camera inside pointed
at the ceiling and chandeliers).
Classical music bombasts.
Oak doors heave wide. The coffin leaves
what's revealed to be a mansion in the woods,
rolling itself into a fresh grave
under bared-slick trees in the rain.
A little metal shovel periscopes up
and starts to fill in the hole.
Crescendo. Fade out. Credits.

Distance, Love, Sum

for Anne

In measure of the hours
we keep, the world
to which we belong
nestled in how it's seen,
there are tracts and versts yet
      to travel. We see
      the materials as they are now,
      not without a story but total,
a hole in the page, in the letter
adrift among stones and firs
on the lonely-line approach to northern towns,
      in a lone onion dome marring the line
      between snow and grey sky, the green signs
      that point to dirt roads, shout Icelandic
      patronymics. Ignore this strength that did nothing,
      forgive the pulsing clusters of subdivision
      that creep as farms first crept, which we cross
      and are perforated by, shot thru with joy.
      The little ruts too, marked with orange
      warnings that precede the rumble of gravel,
          are more in the groove
          of the grandfathered-in hut
          on the back quarter that peaks round
          the manse, that drinks trunk
          highway. There are men
wearing skull masks, who don't see
the ends of their thirst and grant nothing. Again
              you and I know the ache that flares
              with distance, measure time
              by that meter— in the ringing
              industrial park, the engines
skittering thru skies and over roads,
the heat and frosted eyelids. Learn
this distance in the zones we cross
and reset clocks for, and see therein how
we must number and budget a love
before the little lights re-emerge for us.

Common Coin

for Cam Scott

my hands
hair
cruelty
buses
shoes
phones
chairs
stones
meat
garbage bags
discomfort
pigeons
stares
houses
floors
pennies (fewer now)
warmth
parked cars
junk mail
spam
"thank you"
"sorry"
"excuse me"
sleeves
elm trees
squirrels
bladder pressure (not too much)
YouTube comments
looking away
eyelid tics
intestinal pains
the last two months of summer
bananas
thirst
words from Latin
words from Greek
depression
violent death (in media)

fear
bread
bad news
tears
touch
touchability
airplanes
helicopters
climate change
climate change denial
numbness
the sun
the moon
chain-link fences
"bad neighbourhoods"
avoiding crowded public spaces
laughter
salt packets
coffee
churches
recordings of bells
conversations on the bus
legs falling asleep
my breath
your pulse
sports highlights in bars
CIA black sites
secret prisons
federal prisons
Van Gogh prints in apartment hallways
absentee landlords
profanity
cameras on buses
traffic signs
indoor plumbing
my cavities
abandoned warehouses
old, repurposed Tim Hortons buildings
canker sores
nuclear war (at 4 a.m.)

mass extinction
travel mugs
biting my lips
(water bottles, too)
comma splice
Manitoban accents
split infinitives
plants (indoors)
the federal conservative party (these days, ha-ha)
sleeping in movie theatres
son et lumière
gardening gloves
Californian wildfires
Australian wildfires
Canadian wildfires
dog leashes
glass sitting on a nightstand, one-third filled with water
blinking
Quaker Oats
radiators
the "Dean Scream"
"love you too"
ritual
my political stances from one, two, five years ago
reactionary ideas about the decline of Western civilization
"money trouble"
toques (in summer)
toques (worn inside) in winter
a pencil behind the ear
the smell of mulch
window sills
parallax
doorsteps
pulling my hair out
coffee stains on walls adjacent to trashcans
residual light on the inside of my eyelids

Paris Syndrome in New York

Poem: to be determined.
Poem: an archaeology of tomorrow.
Poem: it is sundown in America.
Poem: will I be as surprised
to be alive in a year as I was at thirty?
at fifty? 100? Poem: will I live
to forget this year's snows, should they come?
Poem: a clearing, morning mist,
a dark green forest, a JPEG
of a guard tower, glitched by artifacts. Poem: the last
leaves are falling. Poem: the adults aren't
around to tidy them up. Poem:
some Canadian bohunk at the heart
of empire and world culture
for the first time. Poem: roadrunner in Manhattan,
achieving escape velocity only
if he doesn't look down or back
(the coyote is Eurydice or maybe us.)
Poem: the museums keep us out and history in,
in theory. Poem: inconceivable vs unelectable
so obviously the former wins—
it's not a conceivability contest. Poem:
the future of [declarative verse] is that it has none.

Poem: I'm trying to be discreet but failing.
Poem: language has its own evil
intelligence. Poem like a ninety-percent
unoccupied condo tower. Poem: *sans papiers*
disappeared at Union Street Station. Poem, are we just
your plague rats? Poem, I'm sick
of listening to my own voice, go fuck
yourself and your atom bomb.
Poem, will you remember
my birthday when I'm decrepit?
I'm writing you now, Poem, and reading you out
in a walk-up mansard in Stuyvesant,
to hear and make you over the A.C.
in a friend of a friend's garret
near the former armoury's turrets.
Poem, it's well past midnight.

Poem, tonight Jordan Scott gave a talk
about Guantanamo Bay and played a tape
of an army medic glibly describing "enteral" feeding.
Poem, a young Bobby Dylan has failed
us and we have failed ourselves.
Poem, the world has us
where it wants us. Poem, I'm overcome
by a want for new needs. Poem, I don't even
like milk or molly. Poem, can I ask
if a cartography of nightfall is the best
you and I can manage? Poem, I wish
you were about reading Catullus at the Starbucks
inside Trump Tower. Poem, I have only myself to blame.
Poem, lead us back to the dialect
of nuclear anxiety. Poem,
I remember reading *I Remember*
by Joe Brainard in Battery Park a couple nights ago.
For me, poem, please stick a pin in the future,
be for Catalonia again and for play as play,
stop pretending to be just an engineer of the human soul.
Poem, resuscitate Phil Ochs and stay
true to the memories of regional truths,
be an inconvenient something I'd like to catch
in the Egyptian wing of the Metropolitan Museum.
Poem, I think I know how this film ends.

Poem: the call was coming from inside the house.

3

THE LOST CAFETERIA

Whitehorse, Yukon Territory, New Year's Morning

jesus-fucking hell of a time
to place and brace myself
a pedestrian hours before sunrise
done with backshift
answering calls for - the veterinary after-hours line
- hungover bus drivers taking sick days early
- lonely texan shut-ins with crossed wires
somnambuling home down second avenue
whitehorse an unstruck bell in hoarfrost depths
towards the bridge and paddleboat
and it dawns on me there's been this coyote
trotting along with me for a while
down in the park by the waterfront
and i ought to be cautious
but it's been months since i've seen the sun
so i keep walking   thinking the usual
about friends and exes down south
and i couldn't yell or say hello anyway
with a tongue gone slack
from lack of real live conversationalists
just - the libertarian scotsman on dayshift
who wants me to think
he knows what the american civil war was
all about - the afrikaner i replace some evenings
(a skeleton with cancer in the bones)
- the up-all-hours owner
one leg shorter than the other
from a teenage injury in the mines
drinking health shakes
fighting a strategic withdrawal
as lou gehrig's quakes him
- the woman from mainz
he brings by sometimes
approaching forty with such a terror
you wouldn't believe if i swore it to you

all within the furthest dot on the globe
from where each started
- furthest with daily commercial flights
- furthest from what goes unsaid
(to say nothing
of all those dots that don't make the map)
          best i can figure i'm just off
          dead-centre of the coyote's universe
          it knows where it needs to go
          breaking from the lines we beat
up the robert service highway at a jog

On-the-Job Braining

How to be a body for eight hours.
How to build a better boss. How to accrue.
How to speak softly on a city bus.
How to exploit chaos. How to lift a woman.
How to re-gift the things people give you
in their moments of despair. How to love
a peon. How to identify
as a consumer. How to hear an important
voice. How to take a biology lesson
based around a recently-extinct species.
How to live in fire. How to live on hot dogs.
How to discourse. How to receive a message
from the Government of Canada.
How to monetize human suffering.
How to win and go on winning.

Nightsoil

My title as janitor at a ballet school is "Mister."
This is the propriety of the propertied.
A future Nijinsky smiles and winks at me,
snaps his fingers, points to what's his, what's mine.

Other bodies make mine an amalgam of horrors.
The scrapings sluice into the trap.
I eat my midday snack in the stench and vapours.

I scrub out stains for a modest fee.
An ideal *Europa* on the Canadian prairie,
the pickup-truck bourgeoisie pull up at the shores of Tripoli.
From the passenger's seat, Marinetti calls, "*Forza Italia!*"

His big-wheel hemi disgorges a trophy family.
Pursuit of beauty is the goal, but the effect is of denial.
To transubstantiate one hunger for another

is a matter of power projection. It is a matter of matter,
to dance up into pure aether until your leavings splatter.
It's a matter of rejecting what you can't bear to be.

Ballet school on a Saturday is the fall of white Saigon.
Every day is like Sunday. Every night is *bunga-bunga*.
Call what's left behind nightsoil. Call me Mister Joel.
Please think kindly of me when I'm gone.

Downtown After Dessert

I've taken the bins to the dumpster
and I'm wasting time, mussing around
outside the range of the cameras
the boss might see me goldbricking on.

I'm reading an op-ed on *The Guardian*
about "sweat-shaming" and a jogger
who'd been asked to leave a stateside Starbucks
because of their smell.
      Rancid coffee
covers my shoes: the bins and dumpsters leak.

Across the street, in front of Starbucks, the man
screaming about how he has no money
is screaming to himself, of course:
what the passersby pay him is no mind.
The pigeons coo, too, but not so much as before
the falcon eyries were installed all around the downtown.

There are so many good-hearted people
in the world,
     so many bosses, birds of prey,
Starbucks, cameras, dumpsters.

Spring Without End

Dancing is of no small importance viewed from a hygienic standpoint.[1] Very few persons possess entirely straight legs.[2] Arms even an inch too long will destroy the balance and relation of one part of the body to another.[3] I ate a lot and therefore feel death.[4] Where there is dirt there is system.[5] Fine bodies were in evil plight.[6] All these defects, mortifying for those who have contracted them, cannot be remedied except in their early stages.[7] The development of grace should be the principal aim of instruction.[8] In the correct use of the body, which makes possible a correct use of time, nothing must remain idle or useless.[9] Unless body and spirit come together, the principle will have nothing to do with them.[10] They must thrill to the strength of lithe muscles responding to the bite of their shoes in the resin.[11] Drawn higher and higher, more unstable, closer and closer to the sun's effulgence.[12] Both feet are off the floor.[13] The best thing to do when you're in this world, don't you agree, is to get out of it.[14] Music with feeling is God.[15] I'll have faith in God only if he dances.[16] On landing I was more impressed and enthusiastic than I had ever been before.[17] Corpses lie all around, but how did they get there?[18] I do not eat meat, but today God wanted me to eat it.[19] The Spirit is clean.[20] The aristocrats and the rich people begged me to dance again.[21] I would whisper in their ears: *non olet*. It doesn't smell.[22] Soldiers, secretaries, orderlies, menial staff, and other bunker dwellers began to frolic.[23] They have slipped away, like water down the drain, with never so much as a gurgle of protest.[24]

---

1   Friedrich Albert Zorn, *Grammar of the Art of Dancing*
2   Ibid.
3   Cyril Swinson, *The Teach Yourself Guidebook to Ballet*
4   *The Diary of Vaslav Nijinsky*
5   Mary Douglas, *Purity and Danger*
6   Ernst Jünger, *Storm of Steel*
7   Jean Georges Noverre, *Letters on dancing and ballets, Letter XI*
8   Friedrich Albert Zorn, *Grammar of the Art of Dancing*
9   Michel Foucault, *Discipline and Punish*
10   Yukio Mishima, *Sun and Steel*
11   E. Kelland-Spinoza, *Male Dancing*
12   Yukio Mishima, *Icarus*
13   Margaret Fonteyn, *A Dancer's World*
14   Louis-Ferdinand Céline, *Journey to the End of the Night*
15   *The Diary of Vaslav Nijinsky*
16   Friedrich Nietzsche, *Thus Spake Zarathustra*
17   Adolf Galland, *The First and the Last: The Rise and Fall of the German Fighter Forces, 1938–1945*
18   Klaus Theweleit, *Male Fantasies Volume 1: Women, Floods, Bodies, History*
19   *The Diary of Vaslav Nijinsk*
20   Laibach, "The Whistleblowers"
21   *The Diary of Vaslav Nijinsky*
22   Roberto Bolaño, *The Savage Detectives*
23   Modris Eksteins, *Rites of Spring: The Great War and the Birth of the Modern Age*
24   Ann Barzel, *Ballets Down the Drain*

Cool Universe

This poem will be urbane,
dressed in fashionable, seasonable clothes
set in motion
            on a bicycle, legs grown
swole from all the inclines.

This poem's view will atomize
the passing frames—
            apartment windows
            old sheds, snatches of the harbour
            caught between passing hills.

This poem will be carried on the North
            Sea breeze into a birch forest
thru the natural world's categories
like precision flicks on an abacus
to spiral out beyond the local cluster
            a précis to warm a cold universe.

The Lonely Numerous

The world is having a fire sale.
All banknotes and first-person singulars must go!
The Last Men (sic) keep traipsing
off the roofs of the earth's mighty condominiums.
We line our pockets with them as they fall.

We work as day-janitors in a ministry
at the heart of the continent.
We comb the grit from its chambers.
We kiss the organs of state goodnight.
We coo to ourselves
about what an excellent job we have gone and done.

By backshift we clean social housing
high-rises like cardboard boxes
with air holes punched out, producing
the dead at a well-measured clip.
We keep our heads down all night,
mop the excess from the floors and walls.

Creaking specialists have words sharpened
for when they hold court in their lost cafeterias.
The service has its one good cop
who shakes his head while he delivers the script
for another body bag being wheeled out.
"This is a disaster," he repeats to no one.

We want to crossbreed our neuroses with the rest
among the stacks of folding chairs, the smell
of chemical hibiscus, the breeze on our necks
as the doors we pass thru
gently close and lock behind us.
But nothing seems familiar anymore.
We are lost, and we are all alone.

Tower Block Cleaner

Naming these things
is the love-act
and its pledge.
        /
Patrick Kavanagh

                              i'm here,
janitor inside the cardboard
box where problems
are placed. here, where
the leavings of money,
colonization, tragedies
of the commons meet
management systems
wielded, with good
intention, by specialists,
experts, technocrats. here
where blood and piss
nevertheless accumulate
and the security man itches
for an excuse, laughs at the old
drunks with their pants falling
down. here, with the flickering
fluorescent lights under
which an industrious nana
daily cleans her floor's
hallway, in a tower block
otherwise clogged by garbage
bags, pizza boxes, adult
diapers, sherry bottles
old newspapers, and so on.

here, where the do-goodery splats onto concrete,
a narrow
stream
of words
trickles,
leads
down
towards
the hole
where they
accumulate
in a puddle
to speak
about cast-
off people
and things.
everything tumbles out onto the basement's trash heap, next to
the overflowing dumpsters, inconvenient, constricted,
obscured as the inhabitants' lives. the chute

                  is usually filled up to the seventh floor
                  by mid-week. the facilities department always
                  has fresh staff shuffling in, new temps and supers
                  but never in force. our labour isn't enough
                  to make it a home, just a hold. and that's the point.

Creatures of the Field

Out of place on a Christmas VHS—
a cartoon version of *The Velveteen Rabbit.*
Even at three I wasn't falling for the ending
that the death by fire was no death, no fire
just a magical change, the rabbit becomes real
breaks itself away from the rosy child's bedroom
to live in the forest, watercoloured and wild.

This returns to me in adulthood, a townie
picking fruit for a summer in someone else's paradise.
There's a fire on the other side of the mountain
and the drone of waterbombers overhead
but these cherries won't pick or sort themselves.
I'm daily in a grove with a smiling-dumb golden retriever
who one morning digs a hole by my ladder
that forces me to the ground. I watch
as she uncovers the burrow, the blindness upon blindness
of the baby moles, each like the nubbin of a child's thumb.
They go their jagged way past a vacancy
that is no smile, just the weapons that mark
a mouth among holes that nothing returns from.

Moon Poem for Coleridge

There're kids bouncing around on the bus,
somehow, though it's well past midnight.
That's okay. You have headphones on
and white noise looping. Across the aisle
a couple argues, the boyfriend leaning in
like he's her manager and she's screwed up
some rich lady's order. He's going to cut
her hours next week for it. She won't make rent.

You aren't Superman. You look up at what
is visible of the moon. Some Yanks went there
once, drove around, came home
with moon rocks in their pockets. It follows
that nobody has ever died there. Dead quiet.
Sea of Tranquility. Dust commands the sphere.

You picture yourself aged ninety-nine
bivouacked on the cusp of lunar orbital bone.
Your breath stops. You float up, keeping watch
over your body, the first corpse on the moon.

Something Yet Deserves to Live

He gauges how far the train that followed
his dragged the woman along the platform
last week with a sweep of his arms, Moses
parting the kitchen table's plates and empties.

Committee-vetted language upholds
the distance a transit worker needs to dodge
a breakdown. An Incident. An Emotionally Disturbed Person.
A fated statistic for him, this

his tenth year as an operator.
When I talk some bad-taste bullshit about it
he's quick to stop me. He did feel compassion
for her. What he resents is the eye contact

she made with him before her half-jump,
before some indwelling counter-force pulled
her back to safety a little while longer,
like God's own rag doll. Eye contact like that

of miserable thousands he sees every day
from the train's cab. In a town where all look down,
passing eyes are dared only underground.
Our talk branches back to the village of our births,

the land he and his wife plan to buy there.
I start clearing dishes when he goes to check
on their daughter, asleep in her crib.
Jack Spicer was wrong. Something yet deserves to live.

Rush Our Bus

A man who, beyond the age of 26,
finds himself on a bus
can count himself as a failure.

coming going excruciating
underfunded overworked
jerked stop-stop-start
Thatcher's dead and I'm here
extimacy's a word I've heard
Halitosis Hal and B.O. Barry
tradies immobile in traffic
pressed chunder-arse to face
the working world botulism
tin-crammed passing
ill-loved mall promenade
shuttered Russian specialty shop
cheques cashed Lions Manor
Assisted Living an unsignalled
town-car bougie coupe cuts
a sudden incipient We.

4

SWEETER THRU DIFFICULTIES

Ora et Labora

He'd wanted to fly airplanes.

Grown now, his eyes spend the days
auguring the nicks on his steel-toed boots.
                One falls off the rack, lies
on the floor until morning. He spends his years
on a dwindling trajectory, a shipping clerk pushing carts
full of bandages, syringes, x-ray machine parts
around the county hospital, learning the broken vectors
of work and prayer, marking obsequious time.
                My father's post-work ritual—
        words
for no one, his fists quivering
to point groundward, arms six and thirty at 5 p.m.
every day, a storm inside the master
bedroom after the door slams, shouting
at absent bosses and superiors,
incoherent rage a drafty old house
is too worn down to mute, half-hour diatribes
practising what he should
                and someday surely will say to his tormentors.

Different prayers on Sundays.
The Devil is real, adversarial,
keeps us where we don't really deserve to be,
loots our pockets for change,
makes it rain every long weekend.
Devotion to a long dilution. All struggle
soon to end, a song of heavenly paradise
bringing joy to hurting hearts—
for the True Christian, we are told, life begins at death.

Country drives in the blue '82 Pontiac Acadian afterwards.
Sometimes we idle around the private airfield,
watching Cessnas circle and land.
A doctor took us up once, one of the bosses
he'd cursed. This small-town *noblesse oblige* gift of flight
may have shamed him, but I wouldn't have known then,
four years old and gape-eyeing the patchwork below.

The Berlin Wall, Again and Again

The world was far from life in our Maritime village,
four years old while they sang and danced on
our twenty-two-inch TV. What was it all about?
I wanted to know about library late fees—
if a West Berliner borrowed books from the East
in 1961, would they be in trouble now?

Some local businessman (don't ask which)
bought chunks of the wall a few years later
placed them in the shale lot between the dollar store
and the revivalist hall—
this was supposed to be a big tourist draw.

More years and wrecking balls, box stores,
the end of Mom & Pop. English graffiti
dancing with German on mottled grey
adjacent to box store parking lots.
A tanking economy. The end of history?
The young went west for work anyway.
The wall fallowed, couldn't follow. It fell instead.

His Whitetails at the Northern Shore

Forty-odd years selling vehicles for General Motors
round central-northern Nova Scotia, down dirt roads that curled
into forest hamlets with tiny wooden churches—
over Nutby Mountain, the old highway under
the Folly Lake rail bridge, thru the Wentworth Valley,
Oxford, Springhill, Parrsboro, then home thru Economy
and Masstown on Saturday's last dime of light.

At retirement: a plaque reading "Platinum Dealer,"
gilt-lipped tumblers, the continent's golden outline
on their sides, sixty-five acres and a cabin for hunts
amid sleepy farms and cottages on the Northumberland.
He saw hoofprints and bought.

Years of renos, a satellite dish
for weekends with us grandkids, the time
until he'd hunt his deer always growing.

How he felt about the quad tracks,
the spent shell cases on his side of the gate?
His was the generation that kept the inside in,
but the stands went unfinished. Fences grew
in thickets, strands, haphazard. Walking his domain,
looking for the soft spots in his defences, his worn
fatigues fit like an older brother's
hand-me-downs would have (if the Spanish flu hadn't...)

Weekend mornings, we'd join his foglight rangings
at the northern shore, checking locks and fences,
walking the path along his boundary-stream.

Later, before the estate sale, we came to him
in album pages, among sun-bleached, notable absences.
He was younger there than we'd thought possible,
with beers and bucks on a score of hoods.
His familiar smile betrayed nothing.

Hunting with pals 'til the end, guys he'd sold pickups to,
their sons. Never on his land, never his whitetails.
Never bagged another deer. Bad luck or old age, perhaps
the subconscious deep-down unsteadying his hand?
We cannot say.

A Catalogue Mandolin

Sitting at a rail-siding in the Miramichi
waiting on the freight
schedule's inscrutable will to transport me
onwards to Edmundston, Charny, Montreal.

The woods are a tunnel
of gold-orange-red with arterial
highway overpass for a ceiling.
To hold off the dawn's frost I watch

my teen self drive over the bridge
to my grandmother's house
one last time—a cabin assemblage
that reeks of small animals, the smell

             filling the gaps left
by deep-pocketed homecare workers
and late-stage, early-onset dementia.
I get out of my folks' minivan and see

myself again in the passenger side mirror
six years old, walking alone down the country road
standing on the suspension bridge.
            I see no salmon

only the rusty bones of a bicycle
just below the river's surface, the back wheel
still spinning in the current.

                  I double
back to the ramshackle house,
seat myself at a last thanksgiving
dinner that goes on too long while
her mask of lucidity dips then slips.
I hear the mandolin she ordered

from the Sears catalogue
then forgot about a year before
she's moved to the rest-home.
The mandolin that's handed to me

after dessert, the two chords I know
papering over the silence of missing years.
                    I haven't played since
though I carry the instrument with me everywhere.

It waits with me, exposed
in those childhood woods
for an engineer to release the airbrake,
the next leg of the ride westwards to start,

just out of reach as I shiver
trying to recall every detail I missed then
the melodies it won't play for me
everything that's slipped from our hands.

Bed Leaves Red Fall

North-south, the orchard's
high-density rows are made stately
by dawn's late arrival. Hustle

on the cusp of sun, fingers
kept cold. Late the hour
a grandmother died in, under other trees,

by train tracks, the Miramichi flowing to the sea
four hours closer to Greenwich mean.
Last night, space folded like bin-tags

in a picker's jostling pocket, the promise
of payment at season's end. Rupture
led to coma, to a passage—all flitted

by in sequence. And the news is here,
in the sign of data that buzzes
in your pocket, among the ladders of the other

farmhands walking sideways, stooped
to glean the lowest-hanging apples,
forgotten before in their simplicity.

They resist the frost accrued, cling
then nourish, but for a time.
You are finding out in this moment.

The News

I imagine his head wrapped in bandages
like Apollinaire, like Kenzaburo Oe
imagined his infant son's head wrapped
in bandages in *A Personal Matter*.
There're crow-caws and his voice

falters, choked-off, alien.
Three years estranged submit to four
to eight weeks remaining. My mother says
a deer just walked past the driveway's mouth
that it's getting cold, that they're heading in now.

The Eschatongues

God the end arrives tomorrow I've heard again and again.
Love and terror and bits of white bread
purple robes, Welch's grape juice
in clear plastic thimbles. Up and to church
on time, or else.
What child would want to get smacked around?

God I'm most humble, except for the pride
I feel when I accept you, age seven.
I'm mature for my age, I'm told by grown-ups,
this though is refuted by the snakes in my stomach
as I wait thru the service by the baptismal.

God I keep speaking your name
keep telling the kids at school
they're going to hell, keep listening
as Mom and Dad speak prophecy in their eschatongues
to wrong numbers and co-workers who come once
for tea, never twice to
the oldest house on the floodplain with the portraits
brought down from the attic, their glares that follow
thru the empty rooms of the Victorian two-storey.

God I keep calling your name as we're dragged by our purity
from one hilltop church to another
after a batch of Baptists "let too much of the world in"
(let little pointy-hat witches into the church basement
Halloween party that wasn't supposed to be a Halloween party).

In between comes a year in the wilderness
comes Bible study and church at the kitchen table
Sunday mornings, Mom, Dad, me. Home becomes church
and we encircle the table with our hands, the purple
and yellow tablecloth flowers.

God I keep talking but my fun-sized eschatongue tires
sooner than adult talk of flames and damnation
sooner too than the baptismal's patient waters
so I learn to shut my mouth and look to the ceiling
thru the little waves, until the preacher pulls me up.

"I Saw the Father..."

I saw the father
and the juices flowing from his mouth—
Cronus eating a good, rare steak.

At age four, after dark
I talked to God.
God seemed to answer
with words, without a voice.
The stars above our village
froze in terror too.

█████████ came to my home some nights
to the little writers' club my mother hosted.
█████████ hosted foster children.
Years later the allegations and jail time.
█████████'s church rallied around him and denied, denied, denied.

I read Nijinsky's sanitarium journals
the part where God commands him to eat meat.
I picture Diaghilev on a palanquin
dying then dead in Venice.
I picture God's canines.
I rub my gums.
I spit blood.

God casts off his cloak.
God spreads his sheets.
God picks his teeth.
It is not yet time for his next meal
but God lives outside of time.

Bona Fide Masters

I like the poems I ought to like,
With a force that feels like destiny. It's what's best
for me, I believe. The boss lives upstairs.
He commands me to live my best life.

I write what I think you will like,
glove expectation's hand.
I mind to mine what is mine.
This is the day's cant. I can't unwind.

Never could. I deliver a sermon, a shaggy-dog schpiel,
to a small Baptist church. I am a child,
literally, maybe eight. At six I'd discovered hell.
I would have preferred not to. I'd yet to read Pascal.

Rewind and dissect. Switch to infrared.
Sunday Best is a synonym for fervour.
I do what's required and lead a prayer,
would plead for stigmata if Baptists knew what those were.

I do what's required and read this poem to you.
Please disregard the previous line.
I believe I believe what I say I believe.
I believe now that my beliefs are mine.

Vivisect a true believer's mind.
Peel back the glove's roasted skin.
Kill the child within if it is found alive.
The topic of my sermon is love. I am still inside.

Head in the Clouds

No, they won't tinker
with his mind anymore.
Faith bestows comfort
in this, its death-orientation.
Hands aquiver, his face
comedy and tragedy,
glioblastoma.
It's like bubble wrap
(in his words) in the hands
of a five-year-old, the mind.
On the monitor it was
a black star, tendrils
snuffing out functions:
language, memory,
the smell of purple,
heart and lungs.
I'd like to tell him—
who is dying a year
after early retirement—
anything that comforts,
so I do, but there's no
need. He repeats himself
about Jesus, who he'll
get to meet shortly, with primacy
over departed family.
All my life I never
felt like I knew the *real* him.
Jesus, Jesus, Heavenly Dad,
Holy Ghost, revealed here, now,
a tarp in a patchy back lot
under which little grew.

Patch Work

Culloden? Could be.
Crest: three thistles.
Dulcius ex Asperis:
sweeter thru difficulties.
We were peasants
eight generations ago.

                              Huguenots? Throw
                              in some of those. Race
                              back thru varied points
                              of interest towards

                 three Orange brothers
                 leaving Ulster in 1788
                 for the Canadas.

                         A (fore)Father
                         of Confederation-slash-amateur
                         phrenologist is local flavour,
                         so long after the fact.

              Quick to suggest
              a half-Indigenous great-grandmother.
              Quicker to defend the idea of *terra nullius.*

     What we like to see
     in ourselves: kings, heroes,
     untouchables, all real characters;

magpie genealogists
hoarding shiny things
from across the water,

    gentleman amateurs,
    selective seers
    let loose in the archives
    taking stock of the old stock—

        snuffling at roots
        a forage of fragments
        from the tree of compound folly.

The White Horse

Fearing that his memory will go
before he does, we press on
in the bedside history lesson, wading
into familial etymology.
Here are the words
learned, earned, returned with
from him—

Kilkeel

a fishing town in County
Down   images in my head
of fallen, bronze-age hillforts   (Gaelic:
dún) almost-fjords to hold Northern
Irish commercial fleets—

Scrap

found in bad neighbourhoods,
his father charged him
with a bouquet of them in defence
of the fat-mouthed younger brother,
far-born feuds clenched in small hands
on the sulphur-smelling streets
of their minor port city, New Brunswick—

Orange

rhyming with itself, like Saint John
rhymed with London-
Derry or Belfast, Fenian with Williamite
bullet with sacrament—

Boyne

river of July Twelfth, only
a name to him, me, so many
generations on these western shores,
an idea flowing never the like twice,
same as "Jordan," (no, "Scamander")—

Grandfather

his, not mine, in his sash those days
of marching and prideful lineage,
twice it's said he rode the white horse
at the head of colonial Orangemen.

Here the first and final story ends, exhausted
in the telling by what's eating him.
I see what preceded us both in welcome sepia,
dashing, primal, terrible,
and am for once glad we have learned to forget.

Continental

Montreal, September 27th, 2019.
The man is dead and I am here,
hunched over papers on "A Satyr
Against Reason" in a windowless room
                              a hundred feet
above the street. Street names the same
here and there, Battle of Waterloo,
Duke Wellington, the names of imperial metropoles
mispronounced differently on each "Dell-
High" street forming their own sort of distance.

The man is dead and I am here hours
after we spoke last, my last words
over the phone being the "I love you" repeated
between us during his rapid decline
                              becoming garbled transmissions
as if I were by myself, echoing back
from the opposing cusp of a submerged canyon.

In the streets below today the world
marched as I was asked to march.
Greta Thunberg was there, bringing traffic
to a standstill, here, for a few hours.
Instead I sit alone marking undergrads
who sat at their desks with Rochester.
When I step outside it's to step inside
a phony Irish pub to sit
beneath authentic green road signs pointing to Tyrone and Meath.

                              Word came
its bled-modern way thru the continent's nodes.
"With dignity," "Without suffering,"
"Without losing himself."
On a five-star hotel's wall in green paint
was the dripping sign of the hourglass, the words
"today's inaction=tomorrow's dysfunction."
Today was a dysfunctional one as well,
spiting all prognoses and timetables.
The man is dead, and I am here.

Notes

"After Turner's Stags": While this poem functions as an ecphrasis upon some of Turner's better-known paintings, it also references Lebanese artist Marwan Rechmaoui's installation at the Tate Modern Beirut Caoutchouc, which is a map made of rubber outlining the streets of Beirut.

"Halifax: Colonial Shards": This poem focuses on the Little Dutch Church in downtown Halifax. In the 1990s a mass grave from the mid-18th century was discovered underneath the church, containing hundreds of bodies from a typhus outbreak.

"Historical Drama": Much of this poem's text was taken from the closed captions/described audio of the T.V. show *Vikings*.

"Aubade of the Oprichniki": The Oprichniki were the secret police of the Russian Czar Ivan the Terrible. The white-on-black text of this poem is taken from the lyrics to "Dance of the Oprichniks" by Sergei Prokofiev, from the Sergei Eisenstein's film *Ivan the Terrible, Part II*.

"Paris Syndrome in New York": Some lines of this poem are taken/adapted from "America" by Allen Ginsberg and "The Death of the Shah" by Frederick Seidel. Jordan Scott's project on Camp X-Ray can be accessed at http://lanternsatguantanamo.ca/.

"Nightsoil": Forza Italia ("Go Italy") is the name of Silvio Berlusconi's far-right political party.

"Rush Our Bus": The epigram at the beginning of this poem has been attributed to Margaret Thatcher.

"The Eschatongues": This word is a portmanteau of the word "eschatology" (the theological study of death and the end of the world) and "tongues."

Acknowledgments

Versions of some poems have previously appeared in *Arc Poetry Magazine, The Capilano Review, The Columbia Review, Contemporary Verse 2, The Dalhousie Review, Death Flails, Dusie, EVENT, filling Station, Grain, The Honest Ulsterman, Insight Journal, The Malahat Review, Meniscus, Orbis, Prairie Fire, Scrivener Creative Review, Soliloquies Anthology, Southword Journal, The Spadina Literary Review, The Void,* and *The Winnipeg Free Press.*

With the exception of watercolour painting in outer space, no creative project takes place in a void. I'd like to thank the following folks for their support, camaraderie and friendship, and to apologize to those I have surely forgotten here:

Ronel Amata, Arlin, Brian Bartlett, Carol Baldock, Pamela Beyer, Ariel Beynon, Danielle Bobker, Brieanna, Ryley Bucek, Rachel Burlock, Margaret "Longshanks" Cassidy-Morozov, Janan Chan, Lindsey Childs, Anne Caprice Barayang Claros, Paisley Conrad, Méira Cook, Linzey Corridon, George Dali, James Davidson, Samuel Doucet, Stephane Doucet, Andrew Dubois, Adele Dumont-Bergeron, Kristian Enright, Jase Falk, Miles Forrester, Brad Fougiere, Hannah Foulger, Marcie Frank, Beth Friesen, Paul Friesen, Nora Fulton, Catherine Gerbasi, Lauren Gervais, Ruth Gervais, Matt Gibbs, Ariel Gordon, Hannah Green, Annalee Greenberg, Sissy Hall, Jane Harms, Nikolai Hill, Riley Hill, Catherine Hunter, Michaela Kennedy, Whitney Klassen, Zoe Lambrinakos-Raymond, Ted Landrum, Domo Lemoine, Anna Leventhal, Kahla Lichti, Madelaine Caritas Longman, Georgia MacDonald, Mark Mackinnon, Janis Maudlin, Leo McKay, Alisha McMackin, Andy Morozov, Garry Thomas Morse, Rachel Narvey, Idman Nur Omar, Stepan Ovechinikov, Kevin Pask, Kara Passey, Louis Pigeon-Owen, Macho Phillips, Davis Plett, Prince Poirier, Barry Pomeroy, Stephanie Pooler, Marj Poor, Deanna Radford, Andrew Roberge, Patricia Robertson, Abby Roelens, Louis Rutherford, Barb Schott, Cam Scott, Sasha Semenoff, Manish Sharma, Michael Shaw, Colin Smith, Joanna Sheridan, Nicola Sibthorpe, Sonny, Starla (Dave), Alex Stearns, Jason Stefanik, Jennifer Still, Margaret Sweatman, Simon Thistlewood, Robyn Thompson-Konski, Marc Anthony de la Torre, Janine Tschuncky, Ultralazer, Jonathan Valelly, Bonnie-May Wadien, Kira Williston, Adriana Wiszniewska, Chris Wyman, Jeff Wyman, Jenn Wyman, Morgan Wyman, Cera Yiu, and Teddy Zegeye-Gebrehiwot.

Thanks to Karen and Ashley at Signature Editions for all their amazing support in bringing this book together, and to Clarise Foster for her thoughtful suggestions and editorial work.

Thanks too to my thesis supervisor at Concordia, Sina Queyras, for their belief in my work, ruthless edits, and general badass-ery, and to my readers, Stephanie Bolster and Jonathan Sachs.

A special thanks to the late Andris Taskans, for his friendship, thoughtfulness, and everything he has done for Manitoba's literary community.

Lastly, endless thanks to my partner, Anne Wyman, for her continual love, support, and always-astute proofreading of my scattershot professional emails.

At the age of 21, Joel Robert Ferguson had the words "BOOK PUNK" tattooed on his knuckles, a decision he still stands by. Originally from the Nova Scotian village of Bible Hill, he now divides his time between Winnipeg and Montreal, where he is pursuing a master's degree in English literature at Concordia University. *The Lost Cafeteria* is his first book.

Eco-Audit
*Printing this book using Rolland Enviro100 Book
instead of virgin fibres paper saved the following resources:*

Trees	Electricity	Water	Air Emissions
2	3GJ	1m3	122kg